Poems of Edward de Vere, 17th Earl of Oxford

Compiled by Kit London

Edward de Vere, 17th Earl of Oxford

Copyright © 2017 Kit London

All rights reserved.

ISBN 978-1976195785

NOTE ON THE TEXT

This book consists of the generally agreed upon works that belonged to the pen of Edward de Vere. As best as I can, I have detailed the date of the poems' printing and not composition. He stopped personally assigning his name to his works sometime around 1576. Many other works definitely exist or have been assigned to other authors. Most of the poems are actually song lyrics that Oxford wrote in his late teens and early twenties. Two works of Sir Edward Dyer: "My Mind to Me a Kingdom Is" and "Whenas the Heart is a Tennis Player" have now been re-assigned to Oxford. Those two poems happen to be the better poems in the collection and have been assigned to Oxford for nearly forty years now. Sir Edward Dyer was an acclaimed poet himself and has very few works assigned to him. I have included poems that I doubt to be by Edward De Vere, but are commonly attributed to/with him ("Visions for a Fair Maid", for example. A poem that delves into the Earl's biography). Oxfordian scholars or devoted fans of Edward de Vere would have you believe that he was the author of Thomas Kyd's *Spanish Tragedy*, all of Jon Lily's plays, all of Anthony Monday's plays, all of Thomas Watson's works and Arthur Golding's *Metamorphous* in addition to the complete works of William Shake-Speare. None of those works are found in this collection. Outside the Shakespearean canon, there is nothing to indicate that he was the author of such works aside from a close relationship with those listed above. This is not to say that Oxford may not have been the man behind some anonymous works and the unidentified Ignoto's canon. Especially if Oxford is not the man behind the writings of Shake-Speare. – Kit London.

Edward de Vere, 17th Earl of Oxford

CONTENTS

About Edward de Vere	i
Labor and its Reward	4
I Am Not as I Seem to Be	6
Reason and Affection	8
Desire	10
Loss of Good Name	12
Forsaken Man	13
Care and Disappointment	15
Of the Mighty Power of Love	16
Love and Antagonism	17
Winged with Desire	19
Changeableness	21
My Mind to Me a Kingdom Is	22
What Cunning Can Express	25
Come Hither, Shepherd Swain	27
Were I King	30
Whenas the heart at tennis plays (Love compared to a tennis-play)	32
Love Thy Choice	33
Visions of a Fair Maid, with Echo-Verses	35
When I was fair and young	37

About Edward de Vere

Edward de Vere was born on April 12, 1550 at Castle Hedingham in Essex to John de Vere, the 16th earl of Oxford and Margery Golding (half-sister to Arthur Golding, the poet/translator of Ovid's *Metamorphoses*). In 1562, John De Vere died and left Edward the title of the 17th Earl of Oxford. Soon after, the young earl was made a ward of the court and was placed under the supervision of William Cecil, Queen Elizabeth's chief royal advisor. His daily routine included French, Latin, writing, theology, dancing instructions and cosmography. He would earned a B.A. in 1564 from Cambridge University and a M.A. from Oxford University in 1566. He then took his study to Grey's Inn in 1567 to study law but never earned a degree.

On July 23, 1567, Edward De Vere, while fencing, killed Thomas Brincknell, an under-cook in the Cecil's household. The William Cecil constructed jury ruled that Brincknell, drunk, deliberately ran into Oxford's blade and committed suicide. On December 19, 1571, Oxford married into the newly appointed Lord Burghley William Cecil's family by wedding Anne Cecil. Oxford grew up with Anne at the Cecil estate while he was a ward of the court and, presumably, hoped the marriage would clear the debts acquired from being a ward. Anne gave birth to Elizabeth de Vere on July 2, 1575 while Oxford was abroad touring the European continent. Oxford spent a considerable time in Italy and took to the culture so much that he was now as the "Italian Earl" in Elizabeth's court. Sometime during his time abroad and upon his return to England, Oxford declared Elizabeth De Vere as not his and that Anne Cecil had been unfaithful. Oxford remained estranged from his wife and child for five years. During that time, Oxford would began an affair with the Queen's Maid of Honor, Anne Vavasour. She would give birth to an illegitimate son, Edward, in March 1581. Elizabeth sentenced Vavasour and Oxford to the Tower of London for several months. Oxford was also banished from court. Upon release, Oxford returned to his wife, Anne. Sometime in March 1582, Edward was severely injured and made lame from street clashes with Vavasour's uncle, Sir Tomas Knyvet. Elizabeth granted Oxford's return to court in 1583. Anne and Oxford would have four additional children until her death of fever on June 5, 1588: Lord Bulbecke (died May 1583 soon after birth), Lady Bridget de Vere (April 6, 1584-March 1631),Lady Frances de Vere (dead on September 12, 1587; presumably as a toddler) and Lady Susan de Vere (May 24, 1587- January 1629). In December of 1591, Oxford married Elizabeth Trentham. In 1592, Oxford sold Bilton Hall on the Avon river and by the forest of Arden. Henry de Vere, the future 18th Earl of Oxford, was born on February 24,1593. On January 26, 1595 , Elizabeth de Vere married William Stanley, 6th Earl of Derby after failed negotiations of marriage between Elizabeth and Henry Wriothesley, 3rd Earl of Southampton. It has been proposed *A Midsummer Night's Dream* first recorded performance was at de Vere's and Stanley's marriage banquet. Bridget de Vere married Francis Norris, 1st Earl of Berkshire on April 28, 1599 after negotiations with William Herbert, 3rd Earl of Pembroke and dedicator of Shakespeare's First Folio, broke down. Soon after Edward de Vere's death on June 24, 1604, Susan de Vere married Philip Herbert, 1st Earl of Montgomery and second dedicator of Shakespeare's First Folio.

J. Thomas Looney with the publication of his *"Shakespeare" Identified in Edward de Vere, 17th Earl of Oxford* in 1920 would re-awaken interest in the forgotten Elizabethan Courtier, Poet and Playwright. As of 2017, no play has been identified as being by Oxford, although he received cotemporary praise for his play-writing. All that is known to be written by him are song lyrics and poems that were most likely composed in late 1560s and early 1570s. No mature work has been found published in the Earl's name.

Edward de Vere, 17th Earl of Oxford

Labor and its Reward

From the preface to *Cardanus's Comfort*, Thomas Bedingfield's translation of *De Consolatione* by Girolamo Cardano. (1572)

The laboring man that tills the fertile soil,
And reaps the harvest fruit, hath not indeed
The gain, but pain; and if for all his toil
He gets the straw, the lord will have the seed.

The manchet fine falls not unto his share;
On coarsest cheat his hungry stomach feeds.
The landlord doth possess the finest fare;
He pulls the flowers, he plucks but weeds.

The mason poor that builds the lordly halls,
Dwells not in them; they are for high degree;
His cottage is compact in paper walls,
And not with brick or stone, as others be.

The idle drone that labors not at all,
Sucks up the sweet of honey from the bee;
Who worketh most to their share least doth fall,
With due desert reward will never be.

The swiftest hare unto the mastiff slow
Oft-times doth fall, to him as for a prey;
The greyhound thereby doth miss his game we know
For which he made such speedy haste away.

So he that takes the pain to pen the book,

Reaps not the gifts of goodly golden muse;

But those gain that, who on the work shall look,

And from the sour the sweet by skill doth choose,

For he that beats the bush the bird not gets,

But who sits still and holdeth fast the nets.

Known Early Poems of

I Am Not as I Seem to Be

From *Paradise Of Dainty Devices* (1576)

I am not as I seem to be,
For when I smile I am not glad;
A thrall, although you count me free,
I, most in mirth, most pensive sad,
I smile to shade my bitter spite
As Hannibal that saw in sight
His country soil with Carthage town,
By Roman force defaced down.

And Caesar that presented was,
With noble Pompey's princely head;
As 'twere some judge to rule the case,
A flood of tears he seemed to shed;
Although indeed it sprung of joy;
Yet others thought it was annoy.
Thus contraries be used I find,
Of wise to cloak the covert mind

I, Hannibal that smile for grief;
And let you Caesar's tears suffice;
The one that laughs at his mischief;
The other all for joy that cries.
I smile to see me scorned so,
You weep for joy to see me woe;
And I, a heart by Love slain dead,

Present in place of Pompey's head.

O cruel hap and hard estate,
That forceth me to love my foe;
Accursed be so foul a fate,
My choice for to prefix it so.
So long to fight with secret sore
And find no secret salve therefore;
Some purge their pain by plaint I find,
But I in vain do breathe my wind.

Reason and Affection

From *Paradise of Dainty Devices* (1576)

If care or skill could conquer vain desire,
Or Reason's reins my strong affection stay:
There should my sighs to quiet breast retire,
And shun such signs as secret thoughts betray;
Uncomely Love which now lurks in my breast
Should cease, my grief through Wisdom's power oppress'd.

But who can leave to look on Venus' face,
Or yieldeth not to Juno's high estate?
What wit so wise as gives not Pallas place?
These virtues rare each Gods did yield a mate;
Save her alone, who yet on earth doth reign,
Whose beauty's string no God can well distraint.

What worldly wight can hope for heavenly hire,
When only sighs must make his secret moan?
A silent suit doth seld(om) to grace aspire,
My hapless hay doth roll the restless stone.
Yet Phoebe fair disdained the heavens above,
To joy on earth her poor Endymion's love.

Rare is reward where none can justly crave,
For chance is choice where Reason makes no claim;
Yet luck sometimes despairing souls doth save,
A happy star made Giges joy attain.

A slavish smith, of rude and rascal race,
Found means in time to gain a Goddess' grace.

Then lofty Love thy sacred sails advance,
My sighing seas shall flow with streams of tears;
Amidst disdains drive forth thy doleful chance,
A valiant mind no deadly danger fears;
Who loves aloft and sets his heart on high
Deserves no pain, though he do pine and die.

Known Early Poems of

Desire

From *Paradise of Dainty Devices* (1576)

The lively lark stretched forth her wing
The messenger of Morning bright;
And with her cheerful voice did sing
The Day's approach, discharging Night;
When that Aurora blushing red,
Descried the guilt of Thetis' bed.
   Laradon tan tan, Tedriton teight

I went abroad to take the air,
And in the meads I met a knight,
Clad in carnation color fair;
I did salute this gentle wight:
Of him I did his name inquire,
He sighed and said it was Desire.
   Laradon tan tan, Tedriton teight

Desire I did desire to stay;
And while with him I craved talk,
The courteous knight said me no nay,
But hand in hand with me did walk;
Then of Desire I ask'd again,
What things did please and what did pain.
   Laradon tan tan

He smiled and thus he answered than:

Desire can have no greater pain,

Than for to see another man,

The things desired to attain;

Nor greater joy can be than this:

That to enjoy that others miss.

Laridon tan tan

Known Early Poems of

Loss of Good Name

From *Paradise of Dainty Devices* (1576)

Fram'd in the front of forlorn hope past all recovery,
I stayless stand, to abide the shock of shame and infamy.
My life, through ling'ring long, is lodg'd in lair of loathsome ways;
My death delay'd to keep from life the harm of hapless days.
My sprites, my heart, my wit and force, in deep distress are drown'd;
The only loss of my good name is of these griefs the ground.

And since my mind, my wit, my head, my voice and tongue are weak,
To utter, move, devise, conceive, sound forth, declare and speak,
Such piercing plaints as answer might, or would my woeful case,
Help crave I must, and crave I will, with tears upon my face,
Of all that may in heaven or hell, in earth or air be found,
To wail with me this loss of mine, as of these griefs the ground.

Help Gods, help saints, help sprites and powers that in the heaven do dwell,
Help ye that are aye wont to wail, ye howling hounds of hell;
Help man, help beasts, help birds and worms, that on the earth do toil;
Help fish, help fowl, that flock and feed upon the salt sea soil,
Help echo that in air doth flee, shrill voices to resound,
To wail this loss of my good name, as of these griefs the ground.

Edward de Vere, 17th Earl of Oxford

Forsaken Man

From *Paradise of Dainty Devices* (1576)

A crown of bays shall that man wear,
That triumphs over me;
For black and tawny will I wear,
Which mourning colors be.
The more I follow'd one,
The more she fled away,
As Daphne did full long agone
Apollo's wishful prey.
The more my plaints I do resound
The less she pities me;
The more I sought the less I found,
Yet mine she meant to be.
Melpomene alas, with doleful tunes help then
And sing Bis, woe worth on me forsaken man.

Then Daphne's bays shall that man wear,
That triumphs over me;
For black and tawny will I wear,
Which mourning colors be.
Drown me with trickling tears,
You wailful wights of woe;
Come help these hands to rend my hairs,
My rueful hap to show.

On whom the scorching flame
Of love doth feed you see;
Ah a lalalantida, my dear dame
Hath thus tormented me.
Wherefore you muses nine, with doleful tunes help than,
And sing, Bis, woe worth on me forsaken man.

Then Daphne's bays shall that man wear,
That triumphs over me;
For black and tawny will I wear,
Which mourning colors be;
An anchor's life to lead,
With nails to scratch my grave,
Where earthly worms on me shall feed,
Is all the joy I crave;
And hide myself from shame,
Since that mine eyes do see,
Ah a lalalantida, my dear dame
Hath thus tormented me.
And all that present be, with doleful tunes help than,
And sing Bis, woe worth on me, forsaken man.

Edward de Vere, 17th Earl of Oxford

Care and Disappointment

From *Paradise of Dainty Devices* (1576)

Even as the wax doth melt, or dew consume away
Before the sun, so I, behold, through careful thoughts decay;
For my best luck leads me to such sinister state,
That I do waste with others' love, that hath myself in hate.
And he that beats the bush the wished bird not gets,
But such, I see, as sitteth still and holds the fowling nets.

The drone more honey sucks, that laboureth not at all,
Than doth the bee, to whose most pain least pleasure doth befall:
The gard'ner sows the seeds, whereof the flowers do grow,
And others yet do gather them, that took less pain I trow.
So I the pleasant grape have pulled from the vine,
And yet I languish in great thirst, while others drink the wine.

Thus like a woeful wight I wove the web of woe,
The more I would weed out my cares, the more they seemed to grow:
The which betokeneth, forsaken is of me,
That with the careful culver climbs the worn and withered tree,
To entertain my thoughts, and there my hap to moan,
That never am less idle, lo! than when I am alone.

Of the Mighty Power of Love

from *Paradise of Dainty Devices* (1576)

My meaning is to work what wounds love hath wrought,

Wherewith I muse why men of wit have love so dearly bought.

For love is worse than hate, and eke more harm hath done;

Record I take of those that read of Paris, Priam's son.

It seemed the god of sleep had 'mazed so much his wits

When he refused wit for love, which cometh but by fits.

But why accuse I him whom earth hath covered long?

There be of his posterity alive ; I do him wrong.

Whom I might well condemn, to be a cruel judge

Unto myself, who hath that crime in others that I grudge.

Edward de Vere, 17th Earl of Oxford

Love and Antagonism

From *Paradise of Dainty Devices* (1576)

The trickling tears that fall along my cheeks,
The secret sighs that show my inward grief,
The present pains perforce that Love aye seeks,
Bid me renew my cares without relief;
In woeful song, in dole display,
My pensive heart for to betray.

Betray thy grief, thy woeful heart with speed;
Resign thy voice to her that caused thee woe;
With irksome cries, bewail thy late done deed,
For she thou lov'st is sure thy mortal foe;
And help for thee there is none sure,
But still in pain thou must endure.

The stricken deer hath help to heal his wound,
The haggard hawk with toil is made full tame;
The strongest tower, the cannon lays on ground,
The wisest wit that ever had the fame,
Was thrall to Love by Cupid's slights;
Then weigh my cause with equal weights.

She is my joy, she is my care and woe;
She is my pain, she is my ease therefore;
She is my death, she is my life also,
She is my salve, she is my wounded sore:

In fine, she hath the hand and knife,
That may both save and end my life.

And shall I live on earth to be her thrall?
And shall I live and serve her all in vain?
And kiss the steps that she lets fall,
And shall I pray the Gods to keep the pain
From her that is so cruel still?
No, no, on her work all your will.

And let her feel the power of all your might,
And let her have her most desire with speed,
And let her pine away both day and night,
And let her moan, and none lament her need;
And let all those that shall her see,
Despise her state and pity me.

Edward de Vere, 17th Earl of Oxford

Winged with Desire

From *Philotimus* (1582) complied by Brian Melbancke student in Gray's Inn

Winged with desire, I seek to mount on high,
Clogged with mishap, yet am I kept full low;
Who seeks to live and finds the way to die,
Since comfort ebbs and cares do daily flow,
But sad despair would have me to retire,
When smiling hope sets forward my desire.

I still do toil, and never am at rest,
Enjoying least when I do covet most;
With weary thoughts are my green years oppressed,
To danger drawn from my desired coast,
Now crazed with care, then haled up with hope,
With world at will, yet wanting wished scope.

I like in heart, yet dare not say I love,
And looks alone do lend me chief relief;
I dwelt sometimes at rest, yet must remove;
With feigned joy I hide my secret grief;
I would possess, yet needs must flee the place
Where I do seek to win my chiefest grace.

Lo, thus I live twixt fear and comfort tossed,
With least abode where best I feel content;
I seld(om) resort where I should settle most;
My sliding times too soon with her are spent;

I hover high, and soar where hope doth tower,
Yet forward fate defers my happy hour.

I live abroad, but still in secret grief,
Then least alone when most I seem to lurk;
I speak of peace, and live in endless strife,
And when I play, then are my thoughts at work;
In person far, that am in mind full near,
Making light show where I esteem most dear.

A malcontent, yet seem I pleased still,
Bragging of heaven, yet feeling pains of hell;
But time shall frame a time unto my will,
Whenas in sport this earnest will I tell;
Till then, sweet friend, abide these storms with me
Which shall in joys of either fortunes be.

Changeableness

Per Elizabethan Court Composer William Byrd's Lyric Sheet (1587)
From William Byrd's *Psalms, Sonnets, & Songs of Sadness and Piety.* (1588)

If women could be fair and yet not fond,
Or that their love were firm not fickle, still,
I would not marvel that they make men bond,
By service long to purchase their good will;
But when I see how frail those creatures are,
I muse that men forget themselves so far.

To mark the choice they make, and how they change,
How oft from Phoebus do they flee to Pan,
Unsettled still like haggards wild they range,
These gentle birds that fly from man to man;
Who would not scorn and shake them from the fist
And let them fly fair fools which way they list.

Yet for disport we fawn and flatter both,
To pass the time when nothing else can please,
And train them to our lure with subtle oath,
Till, weary of their wiles, ourselves we ease;
And then we say when we their fancy try,
To play with fools, O what a fool was I.

Known Early Poems of

My Mind to Me a Kingdom Is

From William Byrd's *Psalms, Sonnets, & Songs of Sadness and Piety (1588)*

(Published Anonymously. Formerly Attributed To Sir Edward Dyer in 1813 and with the Rawlinson Manuscript in 1850. Long viewed as Shakespearean, the poem is now consider to be Oxford's due to relationship with Byrd and similarities to his works. Even Anti-Oxfordian Professor Stephen May believes the poem to be the work of Oxford. The poem stands as an oddity, a flashing of unquestionable brilliance, compare to Dryer's other works.)

>My mind to me a kingdom is;
>Such perfect joy therein I find
>That it excels all other bliss
>That world affords or grows by kind.
>Though much I want which most men have,
>Yet still my mind forbids to crave.
>
>No princely pomp, no wealthy store,
>No force to win the victory,
>No wily wit to salve a sore,
>No shape to feed each gazing eye;
>To none of these I yield as thrall.
>For why my mind doth serve for all.
>
>I see how plenty suffers oft,
>How hasty climbers soon do fall;

Edward de Vere, 17th Earl of Oxford

I see that those that are aloft
Mishap doth threaten most of all;
They get with toil, they keep with fear.
Such cares my mind could never bear.

Content I live, this is my stay;
I seek no more than may suffice;
I press to bear no haughty sway;
Look what I lack my mind supplies;
Lo, thus I triumph like a king,
Content with that my mind doth bring.

Some have too much, yet still do crave;
I little have, and seek no more.
They are but poor, though much they have,
And I am rich with little store.
They poor, I rich; they beg, I give;
They lack, I leave, they pine, I live.

I laugh not at another's loss;
I grudge not at another's gain:
No worldly waves my mind can toss;
My state at one doth still remain.
I fear no foe, nor fawning friend;
I loathe not life, nor dread my end.

Some weigh their pleasure by their lust,
Their wisdom by their rage of will,
Their treasure is their only trust;

And cloaked craft their store of skill.
But all the pleasure that I find
Is to maintain a quiet mind.

My wealth is health and perfect ease;
My conscience clear my chief defense;
I neither seek by bribes to please,
Nor by deceit to breed offense.
Thus do I live; thus will I die.
Would all did so as well as I!

Edward de Vere, 17th Earl of Oxford

What Cunning Can Express

From *Phoenix Nest* (1593) Set Forth by R.S.

    What cunning can express
      The favor of her face?
    To whom in this distress,
      I do appeal for grace.
    A thousand Cupids fly
      About her gentle eye.

    From which each throws a dart,
      That kindleth soft sweet fire:
    Within my sighing heart,
      Possessed by Desire.
    No sweeter life I try,
      Than in her love to die.

    The lily in the field,
      That glories in his white,
    For pureness now must yield,
      And render up his right;
    Heaven pictured in her face,
      Doth promise joy and grace.

    Fair Cynthia's silver light,
      That beats on running streams,
    Compares not with her white,
      Whose hairs are all sun-beams;

So bright my Nymph doth shine,
As day unto my eye.

With this there is a red,
Exceeds the Damask-Rose;
Which in her cheeks is spread,
Whence every favor grows.
In sky there is no star,
But she surmounts it far.

When Phoebus from the bed
Of Thetis doth arise,
The morning blushing red,
In fair carnation wise;
He shows in my Nymph's face,
As Queen of every grace.

This pleasant lily white,
This taint of roseate red;
This Cynthia's silver light,
This sweet fair Dea spread;
These sunbeams in mine eye,
These beauties make me die.

Edward de Vere, 17th Earl of Oxford

Come Hither, Shepherd Swain

From Breton's *Bower of Delights* (1592)
Certainly written before 1589.

Come hither, shepherd swain!
Sir, what do you require?
I pray thee show to me thy name;
My name is Fond Desire.

When wert thou born, Desire?
In pride and pomp of May.
By whom, sweet boy, wert thou begot?
By fond conceit men say.

Tell me who was thy nurse?
Fresh youth, in sugar'd joy.
What was thy meat and daily food?
Sad sighs and great annoy.

What had'st thou then to drink?
Unfeigned lover's tears.
What cradle wert thou rocked in?
In hope devoid of fears.

What lulled thee to thy sleep
Sweet thoughts that liked one best.
And where is now thy dwelling place?
In gentle hearts I rest.

Doth company displease?
It doth in many one.
Where would Desire then choose to be?
He loves to muse alone.

What feedeth most thy sight?
To gaze on beauty still.
Whom find'st thou most thy foe?
Disdain of my good will.

Will ever age or death
Bring thee unto decay?
No, no, Desire both lives and dies
A thousand times a day.

Then, Fond Desire, farewell;
Thou art no mate for me;
I should be loath, methinks, to dwell
With such a one as thee.

Fragment of "Come Hither, Shepherd Swain" quoted and assigned to Edward De Vere in *Arte of English Poesy* by Richard Puttenham (1589) Ornament Lib. III page 215-216

> When wert thou born, Desire?
> In pride and pomp of May.
> By whom, sweet boy, wert thou begot?
> By fond conceit men say.
>
> Tell me who was thy nurse?
> Fresh youth, in sugar'd joy.
> What was thy meat and daily food?
> Sad sighs and great annoy.
>
> What had'st thou then to drink?
> Unfeigned lover's tears.
> What cradle wert thou rocked in?
> In hope devoid of fears.

Known Early Poems of

Were I King

Published by Gorsart in *The Fuller Worthies' Library* (1872)

Were I a king I might command content;
Were I obscure unknown would be my cares,
And were I dead no thoughts should me torment,
Nor words, nor wrongs, nor love, nor hate, nor fears
A doubtful choice of these things which to crave,
A kingdom or a cottage or a grave.

Sir Philip Sidney (1554-1586)'s answer:
Wert thou a King yet not command content,
Since empire none thy mind could yet suffice,
Wert thou obscure still cares would thee torment;
But wert thou dead, all care and sorrow dies;
An easy choice of these things which to crave,
No kingdom nor a cottage but a grave.

Robert Greene (1558-1592)'s much later answer with "Farewell to Folly" and a possible reference to "My Mind to Me a Kingdom Is" with the final line:
Sweet are the thoughts that savor of content
The quiet mind is richer than a crown;
Sweet are the nights in careless slumber spent;
The poor estate scorns fortune's angry frown.
Such sweet content, such minds, such sleep, such bliss,

Beggars enjoy, when princes oft do miss.

The homely house that harbors quiet rest;
The cottage that affords no pride nor care;
The mean that 'grees with country music best;
The sweet consort of mirth and music's fare;
Obscured life sets down a type of bliss:
A mind content both crown and kingdom is.

Whenas the heart at tennis plays (Love compared to a tennis-play)

From *Wit's Interpreter* (1685). Originally assigned to Sir Edward Dryer.

(For what reasons this poem was assigned to Oxford in 1935 are not apparent to me. Dryer used the rhyming couplet in "A Lady Forsaken Complayneth" with a meter of eight feet. Perhaps that is why this poem with rhyming couplets of seven feet was assigned to Dyer. This poem, a sonnet, does show a reasoning skill that is displayed by many characters within the Shakespeare cannon. Oxford's love for tennis has been preserved in history due to a 1579 quarrel with Sir Philip Sidney on the tennis court at Whitehall. The event like Shakespeare wrote in Hamlet that two young men had a "falling out at a tennis".)

>Whenas the heart at tennis plays, and men to gaming fall,
>Love is the court, hope is the house, and favor serves the ball.
>The ball itself is true desert; the line ,which measure shows,
>Is reason, whereon judgment looks how players win or lose.
>The jetty is deceitful guile; the stopper, jealousy,
>Which hath Sir Argus' hundred eyes wherewith to watch and pry.
>The fault, wherewith fifteen is lost, is want of wit and sense,
>And he that brings the racket in is double diligence.
>And lo, the racket is freewill, which makes the ball rebound;
>And noble beauty is the chase, of every game the ground.
>But rashness strikes the ball awry, and where is oversight?
>"A bandy ho", the people cry, and so the ball takes flight.
>Now, in the end, good-liking proves content the game and gain.
>Thus, in a tennis, knit I love, a pleasure mixed with pain.

Love Thy Choice

Published by Grosart in *The Fuller Worthies' Library* as "Love thy Choice" Commonly assigned to Edward De Vere. Most likely by Thomas Watson.

Who taught thee first to sigh, alas, my heart?
Who taught thy tongue the woeful words of plaint?
Who filled your eyes with tears of bitter smart?
Who gave thee grief and made thy joys to faint?
Who first did paint with colors pale thy face?
Who first did break thy sleeps of quiet rest?
Above the rest in court who gave thee grace?
Who made thee strive in honor to be best?
In constant truth to bide so firm and sure,
To scorn the world regarding but thy friends?
With patient mind each passion to endure,
In one desire to settle to the end?
Love then thy choice wherein such choice thou bind,
As naught but death may ever change thy mind.

Sonnet LX
Published In Thomas Watson's Posthumous *Tears of Fancy* (1592)

Who taught thee first to sigh "Alas", sweet heart? *love*
Who taught thy tongue to marshal words of plaint? *love*
Who field thine eyes with tears of bitter smart? *love*
Who gave thee grief and made thy joys so faint? *love*
Who first did paint with colors pale thy face? *love*
Who first did break thy sleeps of quiet rest? *love*
Who force thee unto wanton love give place? *love*
Who thrall thy thoughts in fancy so distress? *love*
Who made thee bide both constant firm and sure? *love*
Who made thee scorn the world and love thy friend? *love*
Who made thy mind with patience pains endure? *love*
Who made thee settle steadfast to the end? *love*
Then love thy choice though love be never gained,
Still live in love, despair not though disdained.

Edward de Vere, 17th Earl of Oxford

Visions of a Fair Maid, with Echo-Verses

Published by Grosart in *The Fuller Worthies' Library* (1872)

(This poem was most likely written by another poet and is a mockery of the love affair between Edward De Vere and Queen Elizabeth's Maid of Honor, Anne Vavasour. The poem has been assigned to Anne Vavasour herself in a few manuscripts. Edward De Vere, while separated from Anne Cecil, took Vavasour as his mistress. The raven-haired mistress gave birth to an illegitimate son, Edward, on March 23, 1581. By the Queen's orders, both, Edward De Vere and Anne Vavasour, were imprisoned in the Tower of London for several months. Edward De Vere was banished from court until June of 1583. Romeo and Juliet like fights ensured in the streets for a few months in 1582 between Sir Thomas Knyvet (Vavasour's Uncle) and Edward De Vere. The street fights led to several retinues being killed and an injury to De Vere that left him lame for the rest of his life.)

Sitting alone upon my thought in melancholy mood,
In sight of sea, and at my back an ancient hoary wood,
I saw a fair young lady come, her secret fears to wail,
Clad all in color of a nun, and covered with a veil;
Yet (for the day was calm and clear) I might discern her face,
As one might see a damask rose hid under crystal glass.

Three times, with her soft hand, full hard on her left side she knocks,
And sighed so sore as might have moved some pity in the rocks;
From sighs and shedding amber tears into sweet song she brake,
When thus the echo answered her to every word she spake:

"Oh heavens ! who was the first that bred in me this fever ? Vere
Who was the first that gave the wound whose fear I wear forever ? Vere.
What tyrant, Cupid, to my harm usurps thy golden quiver ? Vere.
What sight first caught this heart and can from bondage it deliver ? Vere.

Yet who doth most adore this sight, oh hollow caves tell true ? You.
What nymph deserves his liking best, yet doth in sorrow rue ? You.
What makes him not reward good will with some reward or ruth ? Youth.
What makes him show besides his birth, such pride and such untruth? Youth.

May I his favor match with love, if he my love will try? Ay.
May I requite his birth with faith ? Then faithful will I die ? Ay."
And I, that knew this lady well, said, "Lord how great a miracle,
To her how Echo told the truth, as true as Phoebus' oracle."

When I was fair and young

Published by Gorsart in *The Fuller Worthies' Library* (1872);
Another extant copy bore Queen Elizabeth's name.

(Like "Visions of a Fair Maid", I doubt a poet would write of themselves in such a manner and doubt Queen Elizabeth is the poet. The poem appears to be song lyrics and never written for Queen Elizabeth to sing/hear while she played her beloved virginal. I disagree with Professor Stephen May and popular opinion that the poem was written by the Queen. The original attribution to Edward De Vere seems more reasonable. Of course, it's entirely possible he's not even the author. The poem has been dated 1583 or prior near the time of the eventual failed courtship of Francis, Duke of Anjou. Oxford was a champion in court, at one time, for the French cause. Pro-Elizabeth authorship proponents claimed the poem to speak of Robert Dudley, 1st earl of Leicester.)

> When I was fair and young then favor graced me;
> Of many was I sought their mistress for to be.
> But I did scorn them all, and answered them therefore,
> Go, go, go, seek some otherwhere,
> Importune me no more.
>
> How many weeping eyes I made to pine in woe;
> How many sighing hearts I have no skill to show;
> Yet I the prouder grew, and answered them therefore,
> Go, go, go, seek some otherwhere,
> Importune me no more.

Then spake fair Venus' son, that proud victorious boy,
And said, you dainty dame, since that you be so coy,
I will so pluck your plumes that you shall say no more
Go, go, go, seek some otherwhere,
Importune me no more.

When he had spake these words such change grew in my breast,
That neither night nor day I could take any rest.
Then, lo ! I did repent, that I had said before
Go, go, go, seek some otherwhere,
Importune me no more.

Printed in Great Britain
by Amazon